(2)

R G MENZIES ESSAYS

ON
FAIRNESS

KELLY O'DWYER,
HENRY ERGAS, REBECCA WEISSER, IAIN DUNCAN SMITH
AND ALEX SCAIFE

EDITED BY NICK CATER

MENZIES
RESEARCH
CENTRE

connorcourt
PUBLISHING

Connor Court Publishing Pty Ltd

PO Box 224W
Ballarat VIC 3350
sales@connorcourt.com
www.connorcourt.com

ISBN: 9781925138610 (pbk)

Cover design by Ian James

Printed in Australia

To every good citizen the State owes
not only a chance in life but a self-respecting life.

Robert Menzies[1]

---

1 R. G. Menzies, *The Forgotten People*, Angus and Robertson Ltd., Sydney, 1943, p. 47.

CONTENTS

R. G. Menzies Essays of Ideas

Sir Robert Gordon Menzies kept a journal throughout his political life in which he would take notes of ideas, conversations and events.

The *R. G. Menzies Essays of Ideas* is published in the same spirit. It does not set out to be the last word on any given topic, merely a record of good ideas, articulately expressed, that may be enriched through further discussion.

If you would like to contribute to the debate online, or submit a contribution for future volumes, email: correspondence@menziesrc.org

Menzies Research Centre

Chairman: Tom Harley

Executive Director: Nick Cater

Deputy Director: Kay Gilchrist

PO Box 6091, Kingston, ACT 2604

Australia

Tel +61 2 6273 5608

Email: correspondence@menziesrc.org

www.menziesrc.org

Opposite: A page from Sir Robert's journal written in the United States in 1948

THE ART OF POLITICS

SUPREME IMPORTANCE OF POLITICS

HARDLY ANY PART OF OUR ...

... INTERNATIONAL ...

THE MOST IMPORTANT ...

THE CONTRIBUTORS

Nick Cater is Executive Director of Menzies Research Centre. He writes a weekly column for *The Australian* and is a regular contributor to *The Sunday Times* and *Spectator Australia*. He is a former editor of *The Weekend Australian*. He is the author of *The Lucky Culture and the Rise of an Australian Ruling Class*.

Henry Ergas is Professor of Infrastructure Economics at the SMART Infrastructure Centre, University of Wollongong, and a columnist for *The Australian*. He was an economist at the OECD from 1978 to 1993, has taught at a number of universities and chaired the Intellectual Property and Competition Review Committee.

Kelly O'Dwyer is Parliamentary Secretary to the Treasurer. She was elected to the House of Representatives as the Member for Higgins in December 2009. She is a graduate in law and arts from Melbourne University and was a senior advisor to former Treasurer Peter Costello.

Rebecca Weisser is a writer, commentator and policy consultant. She was a leader writer and Opinion Editor for *The Australian* from 2007 to 2015 and also edited its popular 'Cut and Paste' column. She previously worked for Qantas and the Australian Catholic University and is a former diplomat who served in Mexico and Vanuatu.

Alexander Scaife is completing a Master of Professional Engineering at the University of Western Australia. He is a Bachelor of Science majoring in Engineering Science and a Bachelor of Commerce (Honours) majoring in Economics. He is a former Mannkal-Menzies Research Centre intern.

The Rt Hon Iain Duncan Smith MP is the UK's Secretary of State for Work and Pensions. He led the Conservative Party in opposition between 2001 and 2003 and is the founder of the independent think tank Centre for Social Justice. In July 2011 he delivered the second John Howard Lecture.

FOREWORD

Building a nation that is both prosperous and just was central to the philosophy of Sir Robert Menzies and a foundation principle of the Liberal Party of Australia. In today's political debate, however, the noble aim of a just society has been reduced to fuzzy notions of fairness and equity that serve as fallacious benchmarks for public policy.

The contributors to *On Fairness* take issue with the premise that fairness and compassion are virtues owned exclusively by one side of politics. Furthermore they contend that ill-considered policies of redistribution and regulation are frequently counterproductive. They result in a static economy with no net increase in wealth in which rich and poor alike lose out.

The Liberal belief in the individual, of the desire of each generation to improve upon the last, casts us in a different position to our political opponents. We see great power in supporting and encouraging people's self-esteem and enterprise for, as Menzies put it, "ambition, effort, thinking, and readiness to serve are not only the design and objectives of self-government but are the essential conditions of its success."[1]

On Fairness lays the groundwork for a forthcoming project which aims to promote the issue of welfare reform to the forefront of policy thinking. Establishing a clear moral argument is central, and Nick Cater does so with great eloquence in his contributions to this volume. The practical case is clear. As Iain Duncan Smith pointed out in his 2011 John Howard lecture, republished in this volume,

---

1 Robert Gordon Menzies, "Forgotten People", *radio talk*, 22 May, 1942.

welfare systems that build dependency destroy hope. Bad systems act as the enemy of many of the forces that motivate self-reliance, self-respect and healthy community structures.

The imperative for fixing our welfare system is not to save money but to rescue lives. The state has a fundamental obligation to protect and assist those of its citizens who lack the resources to care for themselves, but to do so in a manner that encourages dependency entrenches, rather than reduces poverty. Statistical measures of inequality, while important, do not measure the incapacity of people trapped in dependency to attain their aspirations. The examples of community destruction that Noel Pearson brought to the Menzies Research Centre seminar for the shadow cabinet shortly after Tony Abbott was elected parliamentary leader in 2010 had a large impact on many present.

Tony Abbott has had a deep interest in welfare reform throughout his entire political career with a phenomenal grasp not only of the details of the various policy mechanisms but also a profound knowledge of the social impact of each programme.

The politics of reforming welfare is vexing especially in the current political climate. Someone or some group can often be painted as a loser and a benefit once in operation assumes the role of an entitlement – a notion courageously challenged by Joe Hockey when in opposition in his speech "The end of the age of entitlement".

It follows that any case for broad reform needs to rest on a clearly argued moral case which is consistently applied through the policy mechanisms that follow. Many modest reforms in the last 18 months have been opposed in the name of some that may experience an immediate change without adequate acknowledgement of the bigger picture. Hence the need for an overarching moral argument to give reform the force it may need to reshape the machinery of welfare. The aim, as Iain Duncan Smith puts it, is to ensure that no one is discarded and no one is left behind.

They are essential elements to the discussion of welfare. Put another way, Labor has tended to measure welfare entirely in terms of how much is delivered and through which mechanisms – it does not seem to account for the potential and desire of people to change. Giving support that unshackles and supports self-actualisation has to be twinned with the removal of policy measures that stifle those same impulses.

The Howard government stands tall for its policy entre-preneurialism by changing the delivery mechanism for unem-ployment services and many welfare programmes from the government to social entrepreneurs especially NGOs. They became instrumental in the design and provision of many family and other social services.

To me the clearest moral case for reform is found in the disasters wrought on Aboriginal communities through dependency. Driven by good intentions the human cost measured in lives and hopes destroyed are beyond estimate. There is much to be done. We hope this publication helps get that work rolling.

Tom Harley
Menzies Research Centre Chairman
June 2015

INTRODUCTION

The Financial Crisis of 2007-8 had a traumatic effect on the Australian Labor Party from which it is yet to recover. The most serious casualty of this philosophical upheaval was the economic consensus that had prevailed for more than a quarter of a century and tethered Labor to the centre ground. Now, rudderless, the party drifts uncertainly, listing as it scans the horizon for any flicker of light that might guide its path home.

When Kevin Rudd came to power in December 2007 he led a party that was proud to own the economic reforms of Bob Hawke and Paul Keating. Indeed Rudd had been at pains to present himself as a fiscal conservative, going so far as to attack John Howard for his lack of budget discipline. He elicited loud applause in his election stump speech with his straight-faced pronouncement, "I am saying loud and clear that this sort of reckless spending must stop."

Fifteen months later he declared that times had changed. The old rules no longer applied; the financial crisis was an event of "truly seismic significance", he wrote in *The Monthly*. It marked "a turning point between one epoch and the next, when one orthodoxy is overthrown and another takes its place". Extreme capitalism and greed had brought the world undone. "Not for the first time in history, the international challenge for social democrats is to save capitalism from itself."[1]

---

1 Kevin Rudd, "The Global Financial Crisis", *The Monthly*, February 2009.

As it turned out, Rudd was partly right. The financial crisis was indeed a paradigm-changing event, not for global capitalism but for the international Left. In countries in which it held power, the Left embarked on a spree of ill-advised spending. Interventionist government was back in style. In opposition, parties of the Left in Europe attacked governments that attempted to restore order to state finances, accusing them of meanness and needless austerity.

Blame for the crisis was attached to financiers; bankers in much of Europe attracted the level of opprobrium once reserved for asbestos manufacturers. Big banking was the new big tobacco. The Occupy movement rose and fell but its anima lived on turning the struggle against inequality into a full-blown crusade. The transformation was evident in the literary review sections of *The Guardian* and *The New York Times*. *The Spirit Level: Why Greater Equality Makes Societies Stronger*, by Kate Pickett and Richard Wilkinson; *The Haves and the Have-Nots*, by Branko Milanovic; Joseph E. Stiglitz's *The Price of Equality* and his recent follow-up *The Great Divide*.

In Australia the ideology of inequity emboldened those on the Left who had never been comfortable with Hawke and Keating's embrace of deregulation and competition. "If we really believe we are just Bob and Paul's dumb-arse step-kids, we should pack up and go home," Julia Gillard's former speechwriter Michael Cooney told a gathering in London in 2014. "We have to reject any attempt to 'do reform again' … the politics of progressive change isn't like using shampoo – you don't close your eyes, rinse and repeat – no, you open your eyes and confront genuinely new challenges."[2]

The notion that Labor's purpose on earth was to correct

2 Michael Cooney….

inequality was sucked into this philosophical vacuum. Its crudest exponent was former treasurer Wayne Swan, who substituted bankers for miners in his exposition of class war. Politicians had a choice, he said, "between standing up for workers and kneeling down at the feet of the Gina Rineharts and the Clive Palmers".[3]

This unsophisticated, divisive narrative sits oddly in the Australian context where resentment of the rich simply because they are rich has seldom been an effective call to action. As D. H. Lawrence observed in the Australia of the early 1920s, "nobody felt *better* than anybody else, or higher; only better-off. And there is all the difference in the world between feeling *better* than your fellow man and merely feeling *better-off*".[4]

The politics of envy was taken up somewhat more adroitly by Labor's Andrew Leigh in his 2013 book, *Battlers and Billionaires*. Leigh's thesis was that rising inequality "risks cleaving us into two Australias, occupying fundamentally different worlds".[5] It was a thesis he admitted had been drawn from the experience in the United States, where relative inequality is greater and has grown faster than it has in the Australia.

Leigh's book showed that to analyse Australia's social and economic challenges through a prism of wealth inequality is a quirky but ultimately futile exercise in reductionism. As Leigh himself conceded:

> The more I looked at the data, the less certain I became that inequality was an unmitigated evil … inequality appears to

3 Wayne Swan, "The 0.01 per cent: The Rising Influence of Vested Interests in Australia", *The Monthly*, March 2012.
4 D. H. Lawrence, *Kangaroo*, Penguin Books, Harmondsworth, Mddx., 1986, p. 27.
5 Andrew Leigh, *Battlers and Billionaires: The Story of Inequality in Australia*, Redback, Collingwood Vic., 2013, back cover.

be good for growth and to have no substantial effects on crime.[6]

In spite of *Battlers and Billionaires'* assertive title, Leigh stages a retreat from his inequality thesis as the book wears on. He rightly takes issue with Wilkinson and Pickett's thesis in *The Spirit Level* with its audacious links between measures of economic equality and social and physical wellbeing. While the authors may have produced "a heady concoction", says Leigh, "I can't bring myself to swallow it. The closer you get to Wilkinson and Pickett's results, the more fragile they appear."[7]

The efficacy of the politics of fairness relies on the proposition that we are living in an unequal and unfair society. The imperative for government to step in to fix it is greater if it can be shown that the divide between rich and poor is getting worse. While that is undoubtedly true in some developed countries, in Australia it is a questionable proposition. Like most proponents of fairness politics, Leigh is obliged to draw on the measure of relative, rather than absolute inequality. Yet as Leigh himself shows, every economic sub-group in Australia is considerably richer today in absolute terms than it was a quarter of a century ago. We have more of life's luxuries, we live more comfortable lives and we have greater resources to protect us against the friction of everyday life

In 1980 average male weekly earnings were $247.10, the equivalent of $970 today after accounting for inflation In 2013 average male weekly earnings had risen to $1437, making the average male worker $447 better off. In retail, traditionally a low-pay occupation, average pay for women in 1980 was the equivalent

6 Ibid, p. 99.
7 Ibid, p. 99.

of $666 in today's dollars. Female retail workers in 2013 earned an average of $1031.

What's more, many of the items we once thought were luxuries have fallen in price to fit snugly within the budget of everyday Australians. Back in 1980 it would have cost 10 weeks pay for a retail assistant to buy a return airfare to London. Today she or he could comfortably earn the money in two weeks.

The frustrating thing for the fairness crusaders is that Australia is, by any reasonable measure, an exceptionally fair place to live. We cherish freedom, the rule of law and the spirit of egalitarianism expounded in the Magna Carta. Australians enjoy 13 years of free, universal education; income-contingent loans for higher education; free, or nearly free, health care; an aged pension and associated benefits for all who need to draw upon it; a minimum wage that is one of the highest in the world; a progressive tax system; unemployment and other welfare benefits; means tested family payments and more.

Even so the politics of fairness has been the source of Labor's most effective attacks on the Abbott government. Labor's fiscal policy, such as it is, may be reckless, its plans for spending irresponsible and its re-writing of recent history disingenuous. Yet by any measure Labor won the argument over the 2014 Budget, the supposed unfairness of which dominated the political narrative for a year.

Unless Liberals can learn to argue back, the one-dimensional caricature of callous conservatism could cruel the party's chances at the next election. In this volume we attempt to put the matter in perspective and road test some counter-arguments. We contend that Labor's claim for the moral high-ground is entirely illegitimate. The party's track record speaks otherwise. Its progressive agenda, while feigning concern for the poor, is largely self-serving, primarily benefiting the administrative class. The Left's interventionist tendencies in government seldom yield the intended result and are more inclined to entrench inequality than remove it.

Our hope is that this work will contribute to a robust discussion and inspire a counter-attack. For while the fairness argument can prove effective at times, its foundations are far weaker than its proponents imagine.

Nick Cater
June 2015

1

RECLAIMING THE MORAL HIGH GROUND

NICK CATER

For how long is the Liberal Party going to let Labor get away with the absurd proposition that it is the party of "fairness"? This, after all, is the party addicted to spending other people's money; the party that bequeathed an intergenerational burden of debt.

Its shovel-ready projects were a boon for cowboy contractors, but its live cattle trade ban sent the real cowboys broke. It created jobs in the people-smuggling industry, but killed off more than 100,000 jobs in manufacturing industries. It was the party that oversaw renewable energy schemes that enriched merchant bankers and union cronies while electricity bills for the poorest rose by 40 per cent.

And yet, says Bill Shorten, Labor is "the party of prosperity – and the party of fairness". Its mission is "to help those struck down by the shafts of fate … to lift people up, and gather them in". Labor believes in "an Australia that reaches out a caring arm to those in need".[1]

There is nothing accidental about the Left's graceless presumption of virtue. Labor has all but surrendered the economic

1 Bill Shorten, speech notes, National Policy Forum, 7 March 2014.

and industrial ground and become focused almost entirely on social progress. It now seeks to prosecute the moral case for an interventionist state. And it is winning.

The Opposition Leader's response to the 2014 federal Budget resurrected the class-war rhetoric of the 1930s, pitching Labor as the champion of the poor and downtrodden against the Liberals intent on making Australia "a colder, meaner, narrower place". The Abbott government's first Budget would impose "brutal and cruel cuts to hospitals and schools" (it didn't) while tearing down everything Australians have built together. The Liberals, Shorten falsely claimed, would demolish the pillars of Australian society: universal Medicare, education for all, a fair pension, full employment.

Shorten's invective conveyed a parody of conservatism, a version that exists only in the socialist imagination. And yet, in a matter of weeks, Labor had effectively won the argument. The conventional wisdom became that the 2014 Budget was hard on the poor, easy on the rich and generous to multinationals. Labor's story has been adopted without question. When Shorten told journalists that the Abbott government is taxing sick people at the door of the GP surgery, cutting pensions and introducing $100,000 degrees his false assertions were seldom challenged. The Treasurer had become typecast and his reputation was trashed.

Forget Joe Hockey's convivial persona; everybody knows that underneath that jaunty exterior is a flint-hearted, cigar-chomping Tory waiting to get out.

* * * * *

Ben Chifley said: "I try to think of the Labour movement, not as putting an extra sixpence into somebody's pocket ... but as a

movement bringing something better to the people, better stan-
dards of living, greater happiness to the mass of the people."[2]
Today the light on the hill burns with a different glow; fairness, as
the modern Labor Party sees it, is purely a question of money. The
Left's proclaimed virtue is funding; the Coalition's sin is parsimony.
Yet we know through long experience that money cannot buy a
better society. The amount we spend on each child's public education, for example, has quadrupled in real terms since 1945. Pupil
to teacher ratios have halved since the war. Are we getting four
times more value out of state schools? Has halving the class size
doubled the success rate? Many parents clearly think not. In 1947
some 75 per cent of parents entrusted their kids to state schools.
Today only 65 per cent are prepared to do so.

We are entitled to suspect Labor's motives, as it suspects those
of the Liberals. Perhaps they are less concerned about the interests
of pupils than they are with gaining the goodwill of teacher unions.
The iron law of government spending is that those who benefit
first are the people who administer it. The Gonski school funding
agreement will pump more money into state schools, but it is naïve
to imagine it is a victory for social justice. It does not prove, as the
Labor Party claims, that it is on the right side of history. Quite the
opposite, in fact.

* * * * *

The dialectic of cold-hearted conservatism versus caring, sharing
progressivism is mirrored in political debate throughout much
of the developed world. To judge by the titles on display in
Waterstones bookshop in London, five years of Conservatism

---

2 Ben Chifley, "For the Betterment of Mankind Anywhere" ("Light on the
 Hill"), 12 June 1949, in A.W. Stargardt (ed.), *Things Worth Fighting For, Selected
 Speeches by Joseph Benedict Chifley*, Australian Labor Party, 1953, p. 65.

has been a disaster: *Cameron's Coup: How the Tories took Britain to the Brink; Hard Times: Inequality, Recession, Aftermath; Breadline Britain: The Rise of Mass Poverty.*

The kindest thing to say about these books is their authors pick the rotten cherries, selecting evidence that supports their author's conviction that Conservative governments are morally irredeemable. Yet most Britons are in a far better place under the Conservatives than they were in 2010, and the convincing win for David Cameron in May's General Election suggests they know it. Two million more people are in work today than in 2010; 550,000 jobs have been created in the last year alone.

Some 700,000 fewer people are claiming benefits in Britain. The ranks of the long-term unemployed have shrunk by 188,000 in the last 12 months. That's more than the population of Brighton. This time last year they endured an undignified, demoralising existence and survived on government handouts. Today they are either in education or experiencing the dignity of work.

In a rational world, this should break the narrative of hard times, breadline Britain, and the Tories taking the country to the brink. It should demonstrate that liberalism and conservatism are the true philosophies of compassion since the best form of welfare is a job. But it makes no difference; the narrative of austerity, misery and penury prevails.

* * * * *

At the Conservative Party conference in 2002, Theresa May, now Home Secretary, spoke from the heart in a manner that made her somewhat unpopular with her confreres. The next morning she defended herself in a radio interview.

"There was a perception out there that the party was a nasty party, that we weren't caring," she said. "What we need to do as a party, and have needed to do, is actually face up to that fact."[3] Some people might find that language of nastiness difficult, she said. But unless the Conservatives were prepared to see their party not as its supporters imagined it but as appeared to others, it would never move forward.

The success of Labor's faux campaign of fairness is a reminder of an uncomfortable truth. Many voters suspect or are convinced that the Liberal Party, despite its name, is the Australian branch of the Nasty Party. Clearly that is not what Menzies intended. Menzies described "the protection of the poor and the weak, and the elimination of the causes of poverty and weakness" as "the supreme business of politics".[4] Centre-Right governments today are obliged to pay much closer attention to the details of monetary and fiscal policy than Menzies ever needed to do. Yet the imperative for economic discipline is not at odds with Menzies' founding liberal principles. The legacy of today's Liberal leaders, like that of Menzies, should be "a nation advanced in prosperity *and justice*".[5]

We are inclined to forget that the Liberal Party was not put on earth to clear up Labor's mess – although it may so often seem like that. The party's job is not just to balance the books. The Liberal Party is not the political equivalent of the receivers sent

3 Mark Davies, "Watching their words", BBC News online, 10 October 2002. http://news.bbc.co.uk/2/hi/uk_news/politics/2313453.stm
4 Robert Gordon Menzies, *Speech is of Time*, Cassell & Company Ltd, London, 1958, p. 221.
5 Robert Gordon Menzies, "Democracy and Management", William Queale Memorial Lecture, Adelaide, 22 October 1954. Reprinted in Robert Gordon Menzies, ibid, p. 199.

in to salvage a bankrupt business. Liberalism has a much higher purpose – a moral purpose – an emotional commitment of which Menzies frequently spoke, but that today's Liberals seem too timid to discuss.

A strange legacy of Thatcherism and Reaganism is that the Centre Right no longer has the ability to mount a moral argument. It is consumed by the numbers and unmoved by the music. Politics has become a dismal science rather than a principled pursuit; its leaders talk the language of accountants and seldom speak from the heart. By concentrating on the economics of good government, we have failed to condemn the immorality of bad government or inspire our fellow citizens with a message of hope.

It was not always so. Margaret Thatcher was never coy about her moral convictions. Her first reaction on becoming prime minister in 1979 was to quote the prayer of St Francis:

> Where there is discord, may we bring harmony. Where there is error, may we bring truth. Where there is doubt, may we bring faith. And where there is despair, may we bring hope.[6]

Thatcher and Ronald Reagan used morality tales rather than ideological statements or military posturing in their rhetorical campaign against the Soviet Union and its allies. World peace was jeopardised not by nuclear weapons, said Reagan, but "by those who view man not as a noble being but as an accident of nature, without soul":

> It is our spiritual commitment – more than all the military might in the world – that will win our struggle for peace. It is not 'bombs and rockets' but belief and resolve. It is humility

---

6 Margaret Thatcher, Remarks on becoming Prime Minister, Downing St Archive, May 4, 1979.

before God that is ultimately the source of America's strength as a nation.[7]

Rhetoricians on the Centre Right are coy about such language today. They carelessly adopt the Left's heartless talk of "human capital" as if people were merely machines. They are inclined to think of productivity and participation as virtues in themselves, forgetting that the dignity of work and the duty of care are fundamental to the human condition.

In "Freedom from Want," the fifth of Menzies's speeches in the 1942 *Forgotten People* series, he spoke of his commitment to "… a wiser control of our economy to avert if possible all booms and slumps which tend to convert labour into a commodity". He went on to say that the Liberal Party was also committed "to a better distribution of wealth, to a keener sense of social justice and social responsibility".[8]

The phrases "distribution of wealth" and "social justice" sound awkward to our ears coming as it does from the father of modern liberalism. Like a vicar in the pulpit who skips over some of the more awkward passages in the Old Testament, we are tempted to leave those words out. But why? Liberals wet and dry believe government should prosecute the case for a responsible society and frame policy accordingly. "The functions of the State," said Menzies, were "much more than merely keeping the ring within which the competitors will fight."[9]

The Liberal Party is committed to progressive taxation. It be-

7 Ronald Reagan, "A vision for America", Election Eve Address, 3 November 1980.
8 R. G. Menzies, *The Forgotten People*, Angus and Robertson Ltd.' Sydney, 1943, p. 47.
9 Robert Gordon Menzies, "The Forgotten People," radio talk, 22 May 1942.

lieves that the state pension should provide not just the necessi-
ties for human survival but dignity and comfort in retirement. Its
social policies reflect our fundamental human responsibility to
assist those who have fallen on hard times or been assaulted by
brute bad luck. Why, then, have we allowed the progressives to
steal a phrase like "social justice" and claim it as their own?

Menzies for one would not have been prepared to cede the
mantle of compassion to the progressives, or "socialists" he would
more accurately have called them. For Menzies the socialist state
was the very opposite of a compassionate state. It was an enslaving
state, one that robbed people of their dignity, sapped their initiative
and drained them of moral courage. The centrally planned dystopia
he describes in his *Forgotten People* radio talk is chilling; the state
should never be allowed to become an institution:

> … on whose benevolence we shall live, spineless and
> effortless – a State which will dole out bread and ideas with
> neatly regulated accuracy; where we shall all have our dividend
> without subscribing our capital; where the Government, that
> almost deity, will nurse us and rear us and maintain us and
> pension us and bury us.

That is not the Liberal way, said Menzies:

> … we must be not pallid and bloodless ghosts, but a
> community of people whose motto shall be, "To strive, to
> seek, to find, and not to yield." Individual enterprise must
> drive us forward.[10]

Menzies' approach to wealth distribution and social justice
bears no relation to the obscenity we know now as the welfare
state. For Menzies it was possible to recognise the state's

---

10 Ibid.

obligation to assist the poor "without in any way ceasing to insist that the first duty of every man is to do his utmost to stand on his own feet, to form his own judgments, and to accept his own responsibilities".[11]

The Liberal conception of poverty goes beyond the question of ready cash. Like Chifley, it is not so naïve as to imagine that poverty is relieved by slipping the impecunious a sixpence. The statutory definition of poverty devised by the former Labour government in Britain uses income as its only measure; anyone who received less than 60 per cent of the average wage was considered below the line. This crude threshold allowed former prime minister Gordon Brown to boast that he had lifted tens of thousands of people out of poverty. How? Because Britain underwent a recession and average incomes fell while Brown modestly increased welfare payments. Yet the poor he claimed to help were more impoverished than ever. They were still surviving on entitlements and still living lives without purpose; but their chances of finding a job had been considerably reduced.

For Liberals, lack of money is not the cause of poverty but the symptom. Its causes lie much deeper – in the absence of education, secure housing, good health and stable relationships. In a free world, everyone is given the opportunity to prosper; those who do not deserve our charity need help to develop the fortitude required to deal with the friction of everyday life.

When individuals fall into poverty, it is not "the system" that is to blame. It is individual bad luck or bad judgement, frequently compounded by vices, such as drug, alcohol or gambling addition.

---

11 Robert Gordon Menzies, *Speech is of Time*, Cassell & Company Ltd, London, 1958, p. 221.

The handing out of cash cannot cure these human failings, but it has the capacity to fuel them.

* * * * *

When the Menzies Research Centre started to look closely at improving the welfare system last year, it seemed to be just one of many challenges facing the Abbott government – and not necessarily the most pressing. The challenge of structural Budget reform loomed large. Government spending was set on a path that is out of kilter with revenue projections in the medium term.

Fixing the Budget deficit – without raising taxes – will require major reform of the large expenditure items: health, education, defence, and of course welfare. It is somewhat startling to consider that the Centrelink computers are required to redistribute 10 per cent of Gross Domestic Product every year. Welfare – which includes aged pensions and other transfers – accounts for around a third of government spending.

Yet I have become convinced that the imperative for welfare reform is not economic, but moral. Improving our welfare system should never be thought about as a way to save money. To talk of cuts to the welfare system is, I believe, not just unnecessary but morally distasteful. A good Samaritan who encounters someone battered by misfortune has an obligation to spend his last penny to bring relief.

Yet we know that the welfare system is wasteful and inefficient. Worse than that; we know that welfare by its very nature offers an incentive to be poor. Welfare – particularly when administered by the state – increases moral hazard. It offers an affordable path to idleness, devalues enterprise and rewards leisure. When the safety net becomes a hammock it turns surfing off Seal Rocks from a recreational activity into a career choice.

There is no room however for flippancy when it comes to welfare reform. We are indebted to some courageous leaders in the indigenous community for reminding us of the pernicious effects of welfare. Galarrwuy Yunupingu described welfare as "poison". He said:

> ... it is time we acknowledged that government hand-outs
> are a one-way ticket that lead us nowhere.[12]

The real problem with government welfare is not that it wastes money but that it wastes lives. In the last decade and a half, we have learned how to speak about the pernicious effects of welfare in the indigenous community. It is an evil that is blind to ethnicity. The SBS fly-on-the-wall documentary *Struggle Street* illustrates the corrosive effects of welfare and the deficit of dignity it creates.

As liberals we believe in opportunity, in offering everyone – regardless of gender, ethnicity or social background – the right to a fair go and the obligation to seize it.

In so far as the welfare trap limits that opportunity – and it does, in a way that can be transmitted from one generation to the next – we must seek reform. To the extent that welfare provision discourages ambition, saps self-will and offers an incentive to live a purposeless life, it must be changed.

An edited version of a speech to the Liberal Party Mosman branch, 6 May 2015.

---

12 "Galarrwuy Yunupingu issues farewell statement after PM cuts short visit to Arnhem Land', *The Australian*, 19 September 2014.

2

THE POLITICS OF ENVY

HENRY ERGAS

Whatever else Joe Hockey's first Budget may have achieved, it certainly placed fairness at the heart of Australian politics. While the Treasurer is entitled to dispute the validity of many of his opponents' claims, the government clearly worked overtime to ensure that its second Budget is less vulnerable than its predecessor to being cast as unfair.

And no wonder: for the rhetoric of fairness is playing an ever-greater role in the melodrama of Australia's daily politics. The government must learn to manage that rhetoric if fairness is to remain a virtue that informs change, rather than an alleged vice that blocks it.

The centrality of fairness in Australian politics is hardly new. It could, on the contrary, be viewed as an enduring feature of this country's political system. W. K. Hancock's *Australia,* published in 1930, famously summarised the essence of Australian democracy as "the sentiment of justice, the claim of right, the conception of equality, and the appeal to government as the instrument of self-realisation".[1]

---

1 William Keith Hancock, *Australia*, Ernest Benn, London, 1931, p. 145.

While Hancock saw many virtues in the "fair go", however, he was clear-eyed about the dangers of its pre-eminence in the pantheon of Australian political values. Not only was it inherently vulnerable to "selfish interests snatching for advantages in the name of justice", but the incessant pressure on governments to ensure outcomes that were "fair and reasonable" demanded more from governments than they could ever hope to achieve. Yet "having taken orders from their constituents", the politicians were "afraid to tell the country what it has cost", leaving voters "perpetually exasperated because they perpetually pursue a quarry which they can never run to earth". The result, Hancock concluded, was a country in which "government, being constantly overstrained, is constantly discredited".[2]

While those tendencies have been longstanding, so have the mitigating factors. Central among them is what historian A. W. Martin referred to as the "firm bourgeois reality"[3] on which Australia was built, with its stoutly middle class emphasis on material progress and self-reliance, its underlying commitment to family and community, and its mild but deeply held scepticism about public spending and budget deficits. Those values lie at the heart of the Liberal tradition; it is only by appealing to those values that Liberal leaders have ever been able to dilute, deflect and defeat the forces Hancock decried.

Robert Menzies was masterful at mobilising that middle-class value system while broadening it to ever-larger parts of the population. In doing so he changed the balance in the nation's rhetoric. "The ancient question, 'Am I my brother's keeper?' has in

---

2 Hancock, p. 277.

3 A. W Martin *The 'Whig' View of Australian History and Other Essays*, edited by J. R. Nethercote, Melbourne University Press, 2007, p. 69.

modern times been distorted into, 'Is not my brother my keeper?'"
said Menzies in 1954. "That mystical creature, the Government,
which nobody has ever seen, has come to be regarded as the
Universal Provider."[4]

Menzies' emphasis on the dangers of viewing government as
"the first", rather than "the last port of call" was highly effective
in tempering the national mood. Although "Australia is becoming
more egalitarian", Donald Horne pronounced in *The Lucky Country*,
"in some of the things Australians really care about", notably "the
tone of people's relations to each other and in access to pleasure",
it was also clear that the Menzies years had brought "a decline in
egalitarian rhetoric".[5] Sociologist and social critic Sol Encel went
even further, charging that while "the natives worship at the shrine
of egalitarianism", that shrine was, under Menzies, little more than
a smokescreen for deference to bureaucratic decision-making that
"undermines the equality which bred it".[6] As for the new Left,
which took shape in the late 1950s, it viewed Menzies' portrayal of
Australian values as mere "false consciousness", crudely designed
to prevent Australia from catching up with the welfare states of
northern Europe.

Similar accusations were levelled at John Howard, who, to
an even greater degree than Menzies, successfully merged the
traditional language of Australian egalitarianism into the middle-
class values that frame the Liberal heritage, placing distributive
fairness as one value among others. His approach, Howard

---

4 Robert Gordon Menzies, "Democracy and Management", William Queale
  Memorial Lecture, 22 October 1954. In Robert Gordon Menzies, *Speech is of
  Time*, Cassell & Company, London, 1958, p. 203.

5 Donald Horne, *The Lucky Country*, Penguin, 1968, pp. 10-11.

6 Sol Encel, *Equality and Authority: A Study of Class, Status and Power in Australia*,
  Cheshire, 1970, p. 49.

explained in 1999 when the controversy about budget cuts was still intense, was to address "the most fundamental challenges facing Australians today by drawing on their own strengths and values – individualism, a willingness to take on responsibility, the desire for choice and opportunity".[7]

For Howard, these features defined "the Australian character, Australian priorities, in short, the Australian way". They included the "essentially ageless" principle of mateship which Howard defined as "the distinctive willingness of independently minded Australians to help their fellow countrymen and women in times of adversity".[8]

It was those pillars that allowed Howard to reach out to "aspirational voters" whose defining characteristic, he said in 2005, was first and foremost "an attitude of mind". It was an attitude of mind that conformed to what he had long described as his own bedrock commitments: "egalitarianism, strong families, entrepreneurial opportunity, hard work (and the) Protestant work ethic".[9]

However, that rounded view, which emphasises the plurality of values in terms of which public policy must be assessed, has come under increasing threat as a rhetoric has emerged that elevates the distribution of income into a consideration above all others. That the change originates in Labor is beyond doubt. Beginning with the campaign against the GST and then reaching a peak in

---

7 John Howard, "The Australian Way", 28 January 1999, available at http://australianpolitics.com/1999/01/28/john-howard-the-australian-way.html

8 John Howard, "Address to the Second Battalion Royal Australian Regiment, Lavarack Barracks, Townsville, 19 September 1999", Available at http://www.pm.gov.au/news/speeches/1999/ 2BnRAR1909.htm

9 John Howard, as cited in Gerard Henderson *A Howard Government? Inside the Coalition*, Harper Collins, 1995, p. 31.

the assault on WorkChoices, Labor has placed ever greater stress on a politics of grievance in which fairness no longer means a balancing of diverse, often contending, claims and goals; rather, it is collapsed into a single, all-powerful, criterion that holds any policy illegitimate if it seems to make any of Labor's core constituencies worse off.

In the hands of Julia Gillard and Wayne Swan, that sole criterion then metastasised into an unadulterated politics of envy, as Labor came to decry any reform that did not punish the "one per cent". And with the public-sector unions wielding ever more power in the ALP, government spending, instead of being a means to broader objectives, was raised to the primary metric by which political virtue was to be gauged, justified by feel-good campaigns such as "I Give a Gonski".

Labor is not alone, however, in transforming grievance into an art form. Rather, drawing the lessons from the unions' attack on WorkChoices, few campaigns relied more effectively on the sense of grievance than the Coalition's onslaught on the carbon tax and on the cost of living. That escalation, it might be said, is in the nature of democratic politics; however, it could not help but push a bit further the impoverishment of the range of considerations on which our politics relies. To make matters worse, the Coalition, having come to office, failed to make a credible connection between its decisions and the wider spectrum of Australian values, as Menzies and Howard had in earlier years.

The result of that failure has been to strengthen the perception that budget repair is an arbitrary matter of who is forced to bear the costs. It entrenches the narrow focus on the immediate allocation of pain and gain which is unavoidably treacherous terrain, and especially so for this government.

The reality is that our fiscal system is already strongly redistributive: the vast bulk of cash outlays goes to low-income earners, while the vast majority of tax revenue is paid by the better off. Moreover, the system has become more redistributive over time, with top earners' share of tax, and the lowest earners' share of cash benefits, rising.

It is all but inevitable, therefore, that reductions in spending, even if they are gradual, will have some effect on poorer Australians. At the same time, increases in tax run the risk of making effective marginal tax rates inefficiently punitive at the top.

That is not to deny that there is scope to move, with the obvious candidates being tighter means testing of cash transfers and more restrictive access to tax expenditures. Even in those areas, however, reforms carry large potential costs of their own. While there are clearly issues with the means testing of the pension, for example, they would be best dealt with by broadening the means test to include some part of the family home rather than by applying ever higher taper rates to what could prove an ever narrower base. To be sustainable, those higher taper rates would need to be accompanied by reforms that made the retirement incomes of middle-class Australians more stable and secure.

Equally, there are tax expenditures, such as those on super and for negative gearing, that – in an income tax system with sharply progressive tax rates – are inevitably of greater value to high than to low-income earners. Those tax expenditures, however, serve goals that it could be even costlier to serve by other means. If additional tax revenues are needed, it would be more efficient and more honest to reduce our extremely high tax-free threshold, which violates the principle of "no representation without taxation" and allows far too many voters to make little or no contribution for the public services that they then have every incentive to demand.

The opportunities to better structure our taxes and spending do not end there. It is striking that over a quarter of public spending on health and education goes to the top one-fifth of income earners, with the share in higher education being greater yet. A progressive move away from the current funding model for health and education to means-tested vouchers, that could be redeemed by competing public or private providers, would increase efficiency and reduce the burden on taxpayers.

These, it should be acknowledged, are extremely hard choices. They are made even harder by the fact some of them at least would require taking on the government's own constituency. It would be unsurprising if a shell-shocked government, having allowed fairness to become a trip-wire, shied away from the conflict they involve, preferring tinkering at the edges to fundamental re-engineering.

It is a delusion, however, to think that tinkering would buy anything more than fleeting respite. Until the government learns to redefine the debate, as Menzies and Howard so ably did, it will find itself with little room for manoeuvre, corralled by political constraints to the point where its situation could become unsustainable.

As it confronts that risk, it should remember Hancock's grim warning. Australians, he wrote, "have not become rich because of their policies but, being already rich, have been able to afford them". However, Hancock continues, "those policies yield diminishing returns, until at last they may become a positive danger to the national policy which called them into existence".[10]

That point is rapidly approaching. As they say in *Game of Thrones*, winter is coming. Someone should tell the voters.

An edited version of an essay originally published in The Weekend Australian, *9-10 May 2015.*

---

10 Hancock, pp. 127-8.

3

FAIRNESS: SO MUCH MORE THAN A SLOGAN

KELLY O'DWYER

Australians are a fair-minded people. Public policy should be fair. I have a deep concern, however, that fairness is being hijacked as a one-word slogan by Labor and the Greens to encapsulate a very narrow concept. Their aim is to set a Boolean test: whether a budget measure takes more from those with higher incomes than they enjoyed prior to the budget and/or gives more to those with lower incomes than they enjoyed prior to the budget.

The truth is that fairness is a much more sophisticated concept than Labor and the Greens' rhetoric suggests. We need to engage the Australian public in a conversation about the many other dimensions to fairness than the redistributive dimension. That will be critical to prosecuting economic and social policy reform successfully.

First I want to put the status quo in perspective, at least in the context of our tax and transfers system which has been the epicentre of the budgetary debate. Australia has a very progressive income tax and transfer system. ABS data shows that households in the lowest income quintile rely on the government for around 55 per cent of their income. Conversely, households in the highest income quintile receive less than one per cent of their income from government.[1] Many of course would argue this is still too high. Households in the top quintile receive only 2 cents in government support payments for every $1 of income and consumption taxes paid.[2] Those in the bottom quintile receive $2.50 for every $1 in income and consumption taxes paid.

Looking at the income tax system alone, for 2011-12, a sixth of all individuals filing income tax returns paid nearly two-thirds of all income tax. Significantly, the taxable income threshold to fall within that two-thirds was $80,000. Around two per cent of individuals paid about 26 per cent of all income tax. At the other end of the spectrum, 45 per cent of those filing a tax return paid less than four per cent of all income tax.[3] Recently the Organisation for Economic Co-operation and Development found that wages represent only 16.6 per cent of incomes for the poorest fifth of the population in Australia. This is the lowest of any OECD nation.[4]

Many look at how steeply progressive the tax and transfers system is and ask themselves whether it is necessarily a fair starting point in that it places too much burden on too few – especially after taking into account the sacrifices that many people make to be in a position to earn a higher income, the risks they take to do that and the fact that whether someone is in a particular income tax bracket may vary from year to year.

---

1 ABS 6523.0 Household Income and Income Distribution Australia 2011-12 and 6537.0 – Government Benefits, Taxes and Household Income, Australia, 2009-10.

2 Ibid.

3 ATO 2011-12 (Latest available) Taxation Statistics.

4 OECD Household Income Survey 2014.

What's fair?

Simple as a slogan, fairness is multidimensional and complex in practice. To illustrate its complexity, let's consider a hypothetical example of David, who finds himself fighting for his life in the face of a cancer diagnosis. The all-in treatment cost is likely to be very substantial, potentially running into tens of thousands of dollars over time.

Consider these questions:

1. Do you think it's fair that he has to bear these costs? Or do you think, it's only fair for the Australian taxpayer to bear them?

2. Does your attitude change if you learn that David has been paying tax and the Medicare Levy at the top marginal tax rate as a PAYE taxpayer for 20 years and never once turned to the public healthcare system?

3. What about if you learn that he inherited a $5 million estate last year?

4. Does it change if you learn that David was a middle-income earner who chose not to take out private health insurance because there wasn't enough room in the family budget?

5. What if that's because he was squirrelling savings away for his first home or paying for his children's education at an independent school?

6. What if it's because he habitually travels first class overseas to stay in a five-star resort on his annual holiday?

7. Does your attitude change if you learn that David

didn't take out private health insurance specifically because he knew that he would be covered by the public purse?

8. How do you feel if you learn that it's a rare cancer that appears to stem from genetic factors rather than behavioural factors?

9. What about if you learn that it's a skin cancer and that David refused to wear sunscreen? Or lung cancer and David smoked two packs a day?

10. Does your view change if you learn that David had been to the doctor on several occasions and, each time, refused to act on advice to have the skin cancer removed before it spread? What about if he had been to the doctor and the doctor has been negligent in not identifying the symptoms?

11. Does it change if you learn that David is a five year old child?

My guess is that at various times during the past few minutes you changed your mind on the question of whether it was fair for David to turn to the taxpayer. That, frankly, is not surprising because fairness *is* a complex question.

It is not only complex at a micro level; it is also complex at the macro level. There is absolutely no question that fairness involves assisting the truly disadvantaged and marginalised. But it also involves questions of intergenerational fairness. Among other things, it also involves looking at the hidden winners and losers, questions of personal responsibility and reward for effort, and complex transitional questions.

Intergenerational fairness

Labor is fond of describing the 2014 Budget as "unfair". But consider the six budgets delivered by Labor over the period from 2008-09 to 2013-14. From an intergenerational perspective, they were clearly the six most unfair budgets in Australia's history. During that period, Australia's net debt position rose from negative $44.8 billion – that is, net cash of $44.8 billion – to net debt of $202.5 billion in 2013-14. During that period, Labor delivered $240 billion in aggregate in deficits, despite inheriting a budget in surplus.[5] Worse, they put in place a wide range of growth expenditure initiatives that were either unfunded or not fully funded beyond the forward estimates, setting Australia on course for further deficits beyond their time in office. Yes, they faced the global financial crisis in 2008. But they also had the biggest terms of trade tailwind in the nation's history, benefiting from an enormous commodity boom that was never going to endure.[6]

Those budgets and the trajectory they established for future years were, quite simply, an enormous exercise in intergenerational wealth transfer from our children and grandchildren to us. As economic historian Niall Ferguson has stated: "The heart of the matter is the way public debt allows the current generation of voters to live at the expense of those as yet too young to vote or as yet unborn."[7] At the family level, most parents look to build some wealth to leave to their children and grandchildren so that they have an easier start in life. At the government level, Labor took the opposite approach.

---

5 *Mid-year Economic and Fiscal Outlook 2014-15*, Table D1, pp. 266-267.
6 ABS 5206.0 Australian National Accounts, National Income, Expenditure and Product, September 2014.
7 Niall Ferguson, *The Great Degeneration: How Institutions Decay and Economies Die*, Penguin, 2013, p. 41.

The Coalition has taken some steps towards turning the ship around, although we are the first to admit we have a long way to go. For instance, real spending over the life of the previous government grew at around 3.5 per cent per year.[8] Worse, the 2013-14 Mid-year Economic and Fiscal Outlook, released shortly after this government came to office, showed that the growth in spending would have increased to an average of 3.7 per cent beyond the forward estimates.[9] As we detailed with the release of the Mid-Year Economic and Fiscal Outlook in December, the government has pulled back average real spending growth over the current forward estimates period to one per cent per year.[10]

Notwithstanding this, we can reasonably expect the next intergenerational report to highlight that demographic changes will see very substantial increases in spending on healthcare, aged care and the aged pension over the longer term. We can also expect that it will show a smaller ratio of "working age" Australians as the revenue base to fund that growing expenditure. Quite apart from handicapping the next generation of Australians with unacceptable public debt at the outset of their lives, we will also be expecting them to fund a higher standard of living for us than they can ever reasonably expect to achieve. Is that fair?

Hidden winners and losers

One of the great challenges to good policy making is that fairness is too often judged with reference to the very visible winner, rather than the hidden losers. That's one of the problems with intergenerational fairness. Too often, we see today's Australians,

---

8 *Mid-year Economic and Fiscal Outlook 2013-14*, p. 3.

9 Ibid., p. 3.

10 *Mid-year Economic and Fiscal Outlook 2014-15*, Table D1 p. 267.

but forget about tomorrow's. But it's also a problem in other areas as well.

The higher education debate, for instance, has focused on those students who are fortunate enough to attend university and who are being asked to pay a little more. But what about the Australians who have not been fortunate enough to attend university who will earn less on average who collectively will be asked to pay a little less? They are the hidden losers under the status quo, and the hidden winners of changing the contribution mix.

The same phenomenon appears in debates on welfare, where the focus is on the visible "winner" who receives welfare, rather than on the hidden loser who funds that welfare – the ordinary taxpayer whose income is appropriated by the state to fund it. Similarly, on industrial relations, where the focus is all too often on the visible workers in employment without sufficient consideration of whether the policy is fair to the small business owner or the unemployed, or indeed the consumer.

Responsibility and reward

Reflect on the thought experiment we went through earlier about David. How did your mind change when you learned that he contributed to his plight, whether by smoking or by failing to heed his doctor's repeated warnings to go in for earlier treatment? I suspect that on the sliding scale of fairness these aspects pushed you further to the "fairer to require a private contribution" side.

Conversely, when David was a minor who clearly could not have made informed decisions, I suspect you were pushed in the other direction. This reflects another fundamental aspect of fairness which takes into account an element of personal responsibility.

Hence, there is limited community angst about individuals with debilitating injuries who have made every effort to find meaningful employment receiving income assistance, yet far more concern about people in areas of high unemployment refusing to move or take on jobs which are "beneath them".

The flipside of the above is recognition of reward for effort, including a recognition of the many sacrifices and risks that Australians and Australian businesses take to drive themselves and our country forward. Those who work harder and longer should be rewarded. Those who put capital on the line to invest in new enterprises should have the opportunity to earn outsized returns – after all, many who risk capital end up losing that capital altogether. Yes, the whole community benefits because these entrepreneurs and workhorses drive the country forward, but far beyond that utilitarian argument for free enterprise policy settings, ensuring government policy rewards effort and risk-taking is a basic matter of fairness.

Transitional fairness

I'd like to finish by addressing what I think is one of the most complex areas of the fairness debate – namely transitional fairness. All governments need to recognise that people make life decisions, and businesses invest, on the basis of government policy settings. In many ways, no matter how unfair and unreasonable the government policy, people should have some reasonable expectation that the settings will not simply change overnight and that when they do change there will be some form of transitional arrangements in place.[11]

---

11 The increase in the Age Pension eligibility age to 70 years by 2035 is an example of a transitional policy. The long lead in time is in recognition of the fact that people need time and policy certainty from the Government in order to plan their financial affairs ahead of their retirement.

That's why when both Labor and Liberal governments have proposed increases to the eligibility age of the aged pension, government has flagged the change well in advance of the change taking effect with long-dated transition arrangements.

The intergenerational report will no doubt highlight the need to look very carefully at a range of growth areas of government expenditure – including tax expenditures. The debate will almost certainly move to very long-dated policy areas like the aged pension and superannuation. I don't want to pre-empt where that conversation ends up, but I would say that one of the most important areas for participants to address will be how to manage transition arrangements.

For instance, there has already been some public discussion about the assets test for the pension and specifically whether the family home should be excluded. Leaving aside for the moment whether it's the right thing to change that assets test, one of the key questions that advocates of change will need to address is how to be fair to those who decided to overcapitalise in their house over a number of years, possibly decades, precisely because of that exemption for the family home.

Herein lies one of the central challenges in the fairness debate. The millennial generation might consider it fair to remove this exemption immediately rather than over time. From their perspective, that would minimise the intergenerational wealth transfer, so why delay? But a middle-aged family or pensioner might consider that completely unfair because they made a range of choices based on that exemption continuing. At the end of the day, perhaps, beauty is in the eye of the beholder, but fairness is a matter of perspective.

The challenge for government is that it needs to take into account all of these different perspectives, and will necessarily need to make compromises between them.

Reclaiming fairness

The traditional Australian society of decades past has changed. Our workforce and economy have changed. And our population is in the midst of momentous change.

We need to set Australia up for the future. Prosperity is not predestined – the decisions we make today will shape our future.

Reform is essential. But now, more than ever, it is clear that we will only achieve reform if we convince the Australian population that the reform is fair. Not fair in a simple redistributive sense, but fair having regard to principles like intergenerational equity, reward for effort, personal responsibility and policy certainty, as well as a moral responsibility to have a social safety net for those who are truly vulnerable in our society.

All of us who are interested in good public policy need to reclaim the fairness agenda and highlight fairness' many dimensions. We need a more sophisticated and nuanced fairness debate. Unless and until we achieve that, we risk compromising our future.

Speech at the Centre for Independent Studies Leadership Lunch, Sydney, 16 February 2015.

4

THE PITFALLS OF BENEVOLENCE

REBECCA WEISSER

*On great national issues, Government may well be the port
of ultimate resort; but it should never be the first port of call.*
Robert Menzies[1]

Life is not fair, even in a country as advanced as Australia. This
may be the lucky country but it is also a land of droughts and
flooding rains. Accident and illness incapacitates; companies go
broke and people are thrown out of work; the trials of ill health
and the infirmities of old age will afflict most of us while our
demise may heap hardship upon our dependents.

None of these occurrences is unpredictable, at least in a
statistical sense. Over centuries, we have, as individuals, families
and communities, developed systems of mutual assistance to give
ourselves the resources to cope.

Today, however, we are confronted with a disturbing paradox:
most Australians – including the poor – are growing richer, yet
increasingly we are abrogating the responsibility to provide for our

---

1 Robert Gordon Menzies, "Democracy and Management," William Queale
Memorial Lecture, 22 October 1954. In Robert Gordon Menzies, *Speech is of
Time*, Cassell & Company, London, 1958, p. 203.

dependents and ourselves. To make matters worse, government policies frequently discourage people from taking personal responsibility by reducing the benefits and increasing the cost of insurance. Studies suggest that Australia is significantly underinsured in areas such as income protection and temporary and permanent disablement. A report commissioned by the Financial Services Council in 2014 found that six out of ten of those who were uninsured said their choice had been swayed by the expectation government would provide for them if they couldn't work.[2]

The entitlement culture

In 1944 Robert Menzies lamented that "for a generation we have been busy getting ourselves on to the list of beneficiaries and removing ourselves from the list of contributors". He noted the absurdity of taxing savings – a means by which individuals can provision for future liabilities – while increasing Commonwealth welfare and pensions. "I cannot readily recall many occasions upon which any policy was pursued which was designed to help the thrifty ... On the contrary, there have been many instances in which the votes of the thriftless have been used to defeat the thrifty."[3]

At the turn of the 20th century, charitable assistance was the main source of welfare in Australia with state-based pensions introduced in 1900.[4] Since federation, the Commonwealth has gradually increased the number of welfare payments that it makes starting with the introduction of a means-tested, flat rate age and

2 Apathy to Action – understanding consumer barriers to adequacy in life insurance in Australia, commissioned by the Financial Services Council and MetLife, 2014.

3 Robert Gordon Menzies, "The Forgotten People," radio talk, 22 May 1944.

4 History of Pensions and other Benefits in Australia, Year Book Australia, 1988, Australian Bureau of Statistics.

invalid pension in 1908, by Alfred Deakin, which superseded state schemes. No new payments were introduced until the Second World War although Queensland introduced an unemployment insurance scheme in 1923 and in NSW widows pensions were introduced in 1926 and child endowment in 1927.

In 1927, future Labor Prime Minister John Curtain called for a child endowment of 13 shillings and five pence a week per child for families with more than two children but it was the Menzies government in 1941 that introduced child endowment, for a much more modest flat payment of five shillings (50 cents) per week for each child under 16. Although the scheme was extended, the payments were deliberately not indexed which substantially eroded their value over the next 25 years.[5]

In 1945, the Commonwealth introduced unemployment and sickness benefit, superseding the Queensland scheme and over successive decades more and more benefits have been added. This year, the latest budget papers estimate that the Commonwealth will spend $154 billion – around 35 per cent of total expenditure – delivering 40 different welfare payments and 38 supplements to 7.3 million Australians.[6]

While an ever-greater percentage of the population rely on taxpayer-funded largesse rather than their own savings or insurance policies to hedge against adversity, governments are failing to collect sufficient revenue to provision for the liability. In these circumstances, fiscal deficit and debt is inevitable.

More disturbing still, a growing number of moneyed Australians regard withdrawal of taxpayer-funded largesse as the very essence of unfairness, and inflict political retribution on any politician

5 Social security in Australia, 1900-72, T H Kewley, Sydney University Press.
6 Budget 2015-16, Fairness in Tax and Benefits, Welfare integrity measures.

who dares to suggest reducing any benefit. Thus, political timidity entrenches entitlements, imposing a growing burden of recurrent spending on future generations.

Consider a new parent earning up to $150,000, who is currently entitled to claim taxpayer-funded parental leave payment equal to 18 weeks pay at the minimum wage, a tax-free cash handout that totals $11,538.90. The parent is entitled to this regardless of how much parental leave they receive from their employer and regardless of how much their partner is earning. In the public service most employees receive 18 weeks leave at full pay. Some employers go further. The Australian Catholic University, for example, may grant up to one year of paid parental leave with 12 weeks at full pay and up to 40 weeks leave at 60 percent of an employee's salary.

A taxpayer-funded parental leave payment to people already receiving a year's paid parental leave is hard to justify when the government needs to borrow more than $1 billion a month just to service its loans. Yet the Australian Labor Party, which designed the scheme, is criticising the saving as unfair even though it disproportionately benefits the well off.

Taxpayer-funded schemes have other perverse outcomes. Employers, such as McDonald's, are using the taxpayers-funded scheme as a base and topping it up to 18 weeks leave at the employee's salary. It seems bizarre that taxpayers would subsidise the wages bill of a highly profitable multinational, even one with an ambassador as convivial as Ronald McDonald. The commonwealth-funded entitlement, meanwhile, reduces the incentive to employers who do not provide any parental leave, to do so.

One way to fix this mess would be to legislate a minimum paid parental leave scheme equivalent to 18 weeks leave at the minimum wage. Some form of insurance similar to the insurance employers pay for to cover workers compensation claims could assist small or marginal businesses that might otherwise struggle.

Risky business

The expectation that the Commonwealth will provide at times of need encourages imprudence at other levels of government as well as in individuals. Moral hazard – where an individual or agency takes more risks because someone else bears the costs – is a common feature of disaster management and mitigation provision.

Since the Commonwealth contributes between 50 and 75 per cent of the cost of replacing essential public assets such as roads in the event of a natural disaster, state and territory administrations are disinclined to spend their own revenue on mitigation or insuring assets. For example, Queensland did not have disaster insurance, which would have reduced the cost of reconstruction after the flood and cyclone damage that it suffered in 2010-11. Premier Anna Bligh said the cost of insurance would have outweighed the benefit to Queensland, which was no doubt true after the Gillard government paid 75 per cent, and the GST to other states was trimmed, with estimates that Queensland would pay as little as five per cent.

Separating the responsibility for mitigating the risk of natural disasters from those who pay for the damage creates not just moral hazard but physical hazard, potentially putting lives in danger and increasing costs for the community. According to a paper produced by Deloitte Access Economics in 2013, spending as little as $250 million per annum on mitigation could reduce the cost of natural disasters by up to 50 per cent and generate budget savings of as much as $12.2 billion for all levels of government.[7] To realise these savings mitigation funds must be spent wisely and this is more likely to be achieved if decisions are informed by local knowledge. Hence better outcomes would likely be achieved if State and local governments financed and managed both disaster management and disaster mitigation.

Moral hazard applies equally to individuals. In the town of Grantham in Queensland's Lockyer Valley, which was devastated in an extraordinary flood in January 2011, individuals who had insured their houses appeared to have little or no advantage over those gifted new houses by the government, financed by the Commonwealth's Queensland Flood Levy. A costly government intervention delivered a double whammy, discouraging responsible behaviour and encouraging irresponsible behaviour at the same time. Compulsory insurance in disaster-prone areas not only provides an incentive for an owner to move somewhere safer but reduces the burden on the taxpayer if people remain in the area and disaster strikes. Conversely, government largesse after a disaster has the perverse effect of encouraging more people to live in bushfire and flood-prone areas than would do so if they had to pay the high insurance premiums for living in a dangerous zone.

A report from the Asian Development Bank in 2008 recommended that governments should establish comprehensive and compulsory catastrophe insurance and that disaster management should be incorporated into the development planning and project approval process.[8] Typically, governments deal with

7 Building our Nation's Resilience to Natural Disasters, Deloitte Access Economics, June 2013.
8 Earthquake insurance: Lessons from international experience and key issues for developing earthquake insurance in the PRC, Asian Development Bank, Resident Mission in PRC, 24 June 2008.

disaster financing after catastrophe has struck. New Zealand is an exception to that rule that Australia should consider emulating. In 1945 the NZ government established the Earthquake Commission with responsibilities that were later extended to other natural disasters including storms and floods. Disaster insurance coverage in New Zealand is compulsory and paid as part of compulsory fire insurance coverage. States such as California and countries such as Turkey, which don't have compulsory coverage, have a low take up and premiums are high whereas universal coverage in New Zealand keeps premiums low.[9] In addition, the New Zealand government works with international reinsurers to cover losses, which reduces the fiscal burden.

Self-help

The virtue of self-reliance has been recognised in Western civilisation since ancient Greece. Euripides wrote in his tragedy *Hypolitus*: "Try first thyself and after call in God; for to the worker God himself lends aid." The 17th century English politician, Algernon Sydney, coined the modern version of this adage – "God helps those who help themselves" which was popularised by Benjamin Franklin.

Self-reliance and mutual assistance were vital to survival in early Australia. These inspired the movement of friendly societies, which were imported into the Australian colonies from Britain in the 1840s. Societies such as the Foresters, Free Gardeners, Odd Fellows, Druids and the Order of the Sons of Temperance provided not only fellowship and social activities but, in exchange for a weekly payment, organised a range of benefits – many of which

9 Ibid.

are provided nowadays by the welfare state – to help members
cope with illness, unemployment and death. A lodge doctor treated
members, sick pay was provided but decreased after the first six
months, lodge pharmacies helped with the cost of medicine, and
funds were provided to cover the cost of funerals.

Friendly societies were very popular – in 1909 there were 58 in
Victoria alone, with over 1,400 lodges and more than £2 million
worth of assets. By 1913, more than half of all Victorians were
insured by them.[10]

Hospital-based health funds started in the 1930s with the
establishment of the Hospital Contribution Fund of NSW in 1932.
The growth of private health insurance continued after World War
II and became so widespread that by 1972 only 17 per cent of
Australians outside of Queensland (which had free healthcare) did
not have private health insurance. The introduction of Medibank,
providing 'free' universal health insurance for all Australians in
July 1975, was short-lived. The Fraser government, elected in
December 1975, made significant changes charging a 2.5 per cent
levy on income with the option of not paying the levy if you took
out private insurance. The Hawke government however reversed
these changes after it came to power in 1983.

The introduction of Medicare by the Hawke government in
1984 dramatically eroded the incentive to have private health
insurance to cover hospital costs since all public hospitals were
now free. Private health insurance dropped from 50 per cent to
30 per cent by 1999 and the carrot and stick measures introduced
since then, such as the Medicare High Income Levy and the private

---

10 Friendly Societies, *Encyclopedia of Melbourne*, Cambridge University Press,
   2005, emelbourne.net.au

health insurance rebate, have still only succeeded in persuading around 47 per cent of people to take out hospital cover.

The merit of compulsory private insurance, with government subsidies to ensure affordability for the poor, is that it would give consumers a financial incentive to find the best value insurers and give insurers a financial incentive to contract the best value healthcare providers. This would drive improvements in services and put downward pressure on costs, restraining healthcare inflation, which was 4.4 percent over the last 12 months, nearly four times the CPI of 1.3 percent.

With compulsory coverage, risk would be spread as widely as it is under public provision and premiums would be lower. Instead of universal free healthcare, Australians would have universal access to a competitive healthcare market, giving everyone the choices that are now only available to those who have private cover. This would be similar to the system of managed competition introduced in the Netherlands in 2006 which has been so popular that it has consistently been ranked first in Europe on the independent Euro Health Consumer Index.[11] A big part of that satisfaction is undoubtedly driven by the fact that access has significantly improved with waiting times for common surgery dropping by up to three times, down to four to six weeks. Only five per cent of the Dutch waited more than four months for elective surgery in 2010 compared with 18 per cent of Australians in the same year.

If, in addition, all individuals who could afford it paid, say, the first $800 in all health care outlays, they would have an incentive to manage day to day health costs prudently. This has been central to the highly successful Singaporean system where no health service,

---

11 Just Stoelwinder, "Creating a better health system: lessons from the Netherlands", *The Conversation*, 5 September 2014.

no matter how heavily subsidised is provided free, to deter over-utilisation. Singapore's life expectancy is the same as Australia (82.1 years), yet it spends only half as much on health as a percentage of GDP (4.5 per cent vs. 9.1 per cent) and was rated by Bloomberg, as the most efficient healthcare system in the world last year, compared with Australia which came sixth behind Hong Kong, Italy, Japan and South Korea.[12]

The growth of government has also dramatically altered attitudes to providing for old age. Not so long ago, people took pride in declaring that they had funded their own retirement. Now almost 80 per cent of Australians arrange their affairs so that they can avail themselves not just of a pension or part-pension but of the generous benefits that go along with it such as cheaper health care services, medicine and public transport. If people don't have large savings in superannuation, there is a strong incentive to take it as a lump sum – paying off their mortgage or travelling – and then go on the pension. Incentives the government provides to encourage people to save for their old age, such as tax concessions for superannuation in the retirement phase, are unfair to people who have saved for their retirement outside of superannuation schemes. Such people may have far less money and far fewer assets than superannuants and yet pay more tax on their retirement incomes. One solution might be to stop taxing retirement savings but treat all income the same for tax purposes once people have retired.

Ideally, governments should only insure when they have a comparative advantage in doing so. For instance, it makes sense for the government to insure against such things as disability at birth where there is no private insurance market and where, even if there were, it would be unconscionable to punish a disabled

---

12 Bloomberg Best (and worst), 30 November 2014, Bloomberg.com

child because its parents had failed to take out insurance. There is, however, insurance for temporary or permanent disability. The National Disability Insurance Scheme will obviously undercut some of that market as well as providing for those who were disabled from birth. It could well have been easier if the government had simply made disability insurance compulsory and subsidised the premiums of those unable to pay for themselves. Existing insurers have the advantage of having established procedures and the private sector is more assiduous in detecting fraudulent claims, a significant risk in the disability sector.

Taxing virtue

Unfortunately, not only do governments rush in to provide services that would be better provided by the private sector insurers, state and territory governments in Australia actively discourage people from insuring themselves by imposing levies on insurance premiums. For example, NSW and the ACT impose a levy on private health insurance and in NSW, Victoria and Tasmania insurance companies have to partially fund fire brigades, a cost which is passed on through increased premiums. These are effectively taxes on self-help.

Insurance taxes in Australia are considerably higher than in comparable jurisdictions. Out of ten comparable OECD countries, Australia was the only one with double digit insurance tax rates and one of only three that impose a consumption tax (GST) on insurance.[13] A study by the Insurance Council of Australia in 2008 found that Victoria and NSW had the highest rate of insurance

---

13 International Comparison of Australia's taxes, Australian Government, 2006, cited in Australia's Future tax system, Chapter E8-1.

taxes of some 30 countries or states surpassing Germany, Finland, Denmark, Switzerland, the UK, California and Japan.[14] These taxes are also a growing source of State revenue.

Taxing insurance seems particularly shortsighted. In 2008 IPART concluded that these levies and the fire services charges were the most inefficient of all State taxes.[15] More importantly, they increase the incentive not to insure and by decreasing the size of the insurance pool, push up premiums even further. Insurance taxes are also inequitable. Raising the cost of premiums means that fewer poor people take out insurance exposing them to greater risk and hardship when adversity strikes.

By increasing the incentive not to insure, governments take on a greater fiscal liability for themselves. The Henry Tax review found that Australia had high taxes on insurance not just in comparison to other countries but compared with taxes on other products and industries in Australia.[16] In view of the fact that this deters people, especially low-income earners, from insuring themselves, it recommended that all taxes on insurance products, including the fire services levy, should be abolished and that insurance products, like most over services, be subject only to the GST.

But this does not go far enough. Where viable and efficient insurance markets can be designed, governments should facilitate them, because in this area, as in so many others, the private sector is able to operate more efficiently, both because competition eliminates poor performers and because private operators are not subject to the same political pressures as governments.

---

14 Insurance Council of Australia submission, October 2008 to Australia's future tax system, Chapter E8-1.
15 IPART 2008 cited in Australia's future tax system, Chapter E8-1.
16 Australia's future tax system, Chapter E8-1.

The role of governments would then be to operate not as a supplier but as a regulator of a wide variety of insurance markets and to provide assistance through subsidies, where necessary, rather than deterrence through taxes, so that all Australians can insure themselves. That would be fairer to all, both victims of misfortune and taxpayers, and re-ignite the spirit of self-reliance on which Australia was built.

5

TAXES, REGULATION AND POVERTY

ALEXANDER SCAIFE

From the Occupy movement to the campaign to make poverty history, fighting poverty and inequality is becoming an increasingly popular cause. In response, politicians have scrambled to propose solutions to the perceived rise in poverty in OECD economies since the mid-1990s. Many of these proposals involve deepening government intervention that inevitably requires more spending and greater regulation. These prescriptions may be well intentioned, but they will only make the problem worse.

The conventional way of measuring poverty employed by the OECD examines relative rather than absolute poverty. The poverty line is declared to be half the median national household income. By this measure, the poverty rate across OECD economies increased from 10.1 percent to 11.7 percent between 1995 and 2011. Many countries have seen even more significant changes, with Sweden's poverty rate jumping from 3.7 percent to 9.7 percent. There are substantial differences in poverty rates from country to country within the OECD ranging from 20.9 percent in Israel to 6 percent in Denmark, variations that are likely to reflect different policies and institutions.

Much of the discussion around poverty has centred on the level of taxation and spending, a narrow view of the issue that lends itself to simplistic and ineffective solutions. Proponents of passive welfare argue that transfers from the rich to the poor are the simplest ways of reducing poverty. This assumes, however, that the level of economic activity is unaffected by the taxes and spending. If the level of economic activity is taken as given, increasing transfer payments to those below the poverty line will undoubtedly alleviate poverty for some in the short term. However, the more that a government taxes, the more it distorts activity in the private sector and the greater the negative effects on economic growth. In the longer term, therefore, social welfare spending may have the perverse effect of increasing the level of poverty.

Economic growth is key both to job creation and rising wages, which is especially important for low-income earners whose income is largely determined by wage earnings. In the long run, economic growth raises incomes for the poorest members of society just as much as for the rich, according to World Bank economists David Dollar and Aart Kraay. They also found that reducing the size of government not only increases growth but also increases the income share of the poorest fifth of society.[1]

Fewer regulations, more jobs

Regulation is rarely mentioned in the context of poverty, but it pays a critical role in how governments impact and control the economy. Figure 1 demonstrates the link between the extent of regulation and the poverty rate for sixteen OECD economies.

---

1 Dollar, David & Kraay, Aart, 2001. "Growth is good for the poor," Policy Research Working Paper Series 2587, The World Bank. https://ideas.repec.org/p/wbk/wbrwps/2587.html

Figure 1: Regulation and Poverty

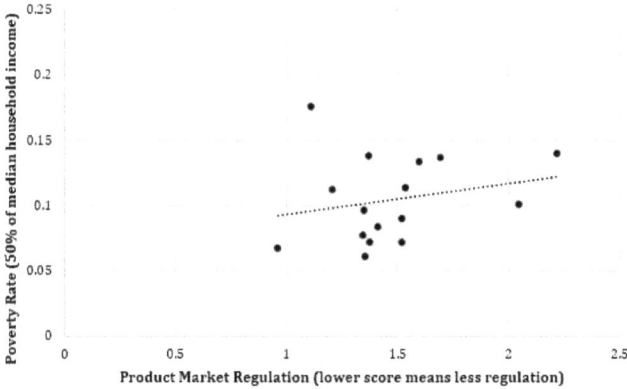

The Product Market Regulation indicator measures the degree to which policies promote or inhibit competition across the economy and includes the degree of state control and barriers to entrepreneurship. A higher score indicates more government oversight of the economy and, as can be seen in the graph, is associated with a higher poverty rate.

Figure 2 establishes a relationship between the difficulty of setting up a business and the poverty rate. When it is harder to

Figure 2: Number of procedures for setting up a business

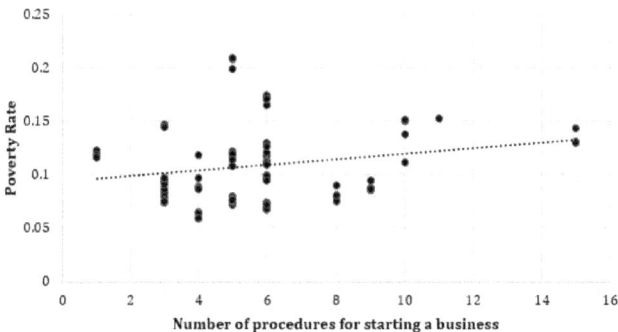

On Fairness

Figure 3: Cost of business start up

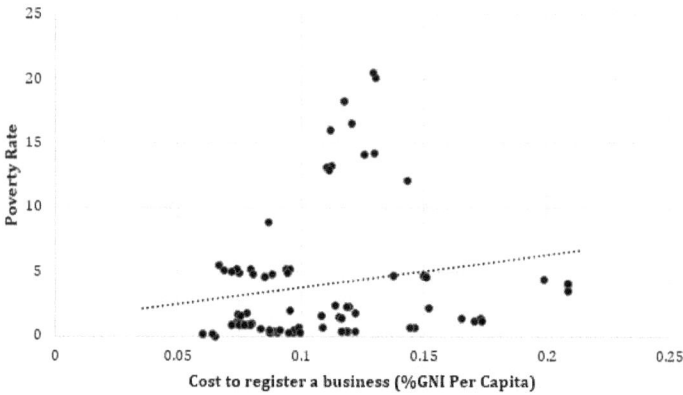

start a business due to increased regulation and bureaucracy, the level of poverty in an economy is generally higher.

Figure 3 displays how an increase in the cost of registering a business is linked with a higher poverty rate. To normalise the cost of business start-up procedures, they are presented as a percentage of gross national income per capita.

Regulation and bureaucracy appear to have significant negative effects on the level of poverty in many developed economies. This is most likely because government regulations and bureaucracy absorb the resources of private individuals and businesses and prevent resources from being used in the most efficient manner.

Job creation

Since the primary engine of job creation is business, the starting point for government should be to create an environment that allows business to thrive. Governments can and do play a vital role in assisting businesses by ensuring that private property rights and the rule of law are respected and by providing infrastructure such as roads and ports. A large bureaucracy and complex regulation, on the other hand, will hamper job creation by increasing costs and erecting barriers to business expansion. This administrative burden can also deter new businesses from forming.

Inflexible or costly rules to control hiring and firing are likely to be an obstacle to employment meaning that economies that have strict labour market regulations having higher unemployment. In a rigid labour market it becomes difficult for an unemployed person to find work because regulations add to the cost of recruitment. Over time it is likely to widen the qualifications gap between the unemployed and the employed, producing persistent long-term unemployment and increasing dependence on social security.

Rent-seeking and regulatory capture are consequences of regulation that are often overlooked. Rent-seeking occurs when individuals or businesses obtain a share of wealth already created without creating any new wealth themselves. The more regulation and bureaucracy there is, the higher the returns from rent seeking.

Businesses can lobby governments to impose regulations on competitors or erect barriers to entry in order to increase their own market share. Bureaucrats can solicit bribes for using their authority to award benefits. The larger and more complex the bureaucracy, the easier this process becomes. When economists Ismail Cole and Arshad Chawdhry compared a number of American states according to levels of rent-seeking activity, measured by the size of government bureaucracies and number of special interest groups or lobbyists, they found these factors retard economic growth.[2]

---

2 M.Cole, Ismail and M., Arshad Chawdhry, (2002), Rent Seeking and Economic Growth: Evidence from a Panel of U.S. States, *Cato Journal*, 22, issue 2, pp. 211-228, http://EconPapers.repec.org/RePEc:cto:journl:v:22:y:2002:i: 2: pp:211-228.

Regulatory capture occurs when an agency that is designed to act in the public interest instead advances the concerns of special interest groups. Not only does it foster rent-seeking but it reduces the effectiveness of governance. When bureaucrats are seen to have greater discretion in the issuing of permits, irrespective of the public interest, increased uncertainty deters new entrants to the market.

Together these factors can substantially reduce the overall ability to invest, which in turn reduces competition, raises prices and leads more households to fall below the poverty line. The larger the size of government bureaucracy, the more likely it is that firms will divert resources from creating employment opportunities and increasing wages towards compliance and the manipulation of government regulation.

Foreign direct investment

Higher levels of foreign investment lead to higher levels of economic activity. Figure 4 shows the positive relationship between restrictions on foreign direct investment and the poverty rate. This is hardly surprising since restricting investment inevitably reduces the injection of finance that would otherwise increase economic opportunities. Restricting foreign investment can also damage market confidence; the willingness of overseas investors to put their money where their mouth is sends a signal to other investors that the country's economy is likely to expand and that they too should invest to capitalise on future prosperity.

A liberal approach to reducing poverty

It is clear that poverty is unlikely to be reduced by regulation and redistribution. Reforms of deregulation and increasing economic

Figure 4: FDI Restrictions

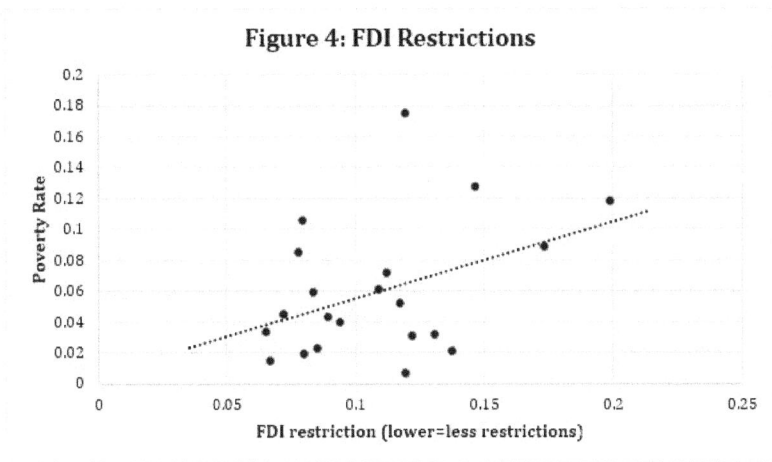

activity are not only good for business but generally prove to be a better way to help the poor. The war on poverty, as some like to call it, should be fought by:

- Lowering the costs of doing business by lowering minimum capital requirements for starting a business and simplifying the procedures for firm entry and exit.

- Making labour markets more flexible by reducing the costs of firing workers and introducing non-standard contracts.

- Linking welfare benefits with employment and work, thus increasing incentives to join the labour force and rewarding gainful employment.

Increasing the size of government is the wrong response to the perceived growth of poverty across the OECD. Imposing more government control over economies, particularly those already suffering from large bureaucracies and burdensome regulation, will have a detrimental effect on economic growth and cause poverty to increase. Governments should instead make it easier for businesses to create jobs by removing rigidities in the labour market, lowering the costs of starting a business, and tying welfare benefits to employment. Only by joining the labour market can individuals free themselves from dependence and poverty.

This contribution was originally appeared in Policy, *Vol. 30, No. 4, and is republished courtesy of the Centre for Independent Studies.*

6

Conservatives and Social Justice

Iain Duncan Smith

During my time as Conservative leader I began to turn the party's attention to people left behind by society. Despite then being the world's fourth largest economy, Britain was constrained by some very deep social problems. Educational inequality was a scar on our society; our poorest children were being failed by the institutions designed to give them a future.

Crime was high and the fear of crime higher still. People lived in growing uncertainty as they walked the streets and tried to get on with their lives, particularly in deprived neighbourhoods. An OECD report looked at our children's wellbeing and found the UK in poor shape. And too many social housing estates had become "no go areas" for police officers but rich hunting grounds for drug dealers, street gang recruiters and violent money lenders.

It seemed obvious to me that those on the centre-right had a responsibility to enter these debates, and help to find solutions. For too long Conservatives had left this area to the left, only occasionally making forays to attack spending on welfare. Everything was viewed through the lens of saving money or catching scroungers, or should I say bludgers.

Yet whilst this might encourage the dyed in the wool Conservative supporter, it remained a wholly negative message and allowed the left to characterise Conservatives as simply interested in cutting benefits. The more I looked at this, the more I believed that this caricature needed to be changed.

The history of the Conservative Party in the UK has always been one of social reform. What else would you expect from the Party of Wilberforce, Shaftesbury, Disraeli and Churchill? Conservatives have every right and motivation to have concerns about the social fabric of their nation. It is in the DNA of Conservatives to believe instinctively in aspiration and mobility. Why then wouldn't we, when we look at the large numbers of people trapped in dependency, want to change that to help them improve the quality of their lives and those of their children? The left's narrow measurement for social concern rests on the amount of money spent. It should be a Conservative obligation to change that test to what money is spent on, and importantly what life change it achieves.

So there is a Conservative philosophical reason to be focussed on poverty. But there is, as ever, another good reason. Such problems demand our attention for economic reasons too. The cost of such social failure drives high and rising public expenditure. In the last decade or so working-age welfare expenditure has increased by some 50 per cent – and that during a period of growth. Over a similar period police expenditure had risen by 50 per cent in real terms and spending on prisons by a third.

Britain has been spending more and more money trying to tackle the effects of poverty, through a growing state, yet the outcomes are poor. For Conservatives who believe in a healthy economy, it is not enough to simply dismiss poverty as someone else's problem – or even a problem for those on the left of politics to deal with.

Even in the rhetoric of the debates many had become paralysed, lost or they had given up altogether. Consider the very concept of social justice for example. I recall people in the Conservative Party having maddening Hayekian debates about how the idea of social justice was a contradiction, as "social" was collective and "justice" individual. Conservatives love nothing more than a good argument about the meaning of words.

But these terminology arguments were utterly detached from the British people, and they marginalised Conservatives even further in the eyes of the electorate. We asked through a series of polls what the term "social justice" meant to the public. Interestingly, they had a much more generalised sense of what the phrase meant. They rejected the notion that it meant a bigger state or increased spending on welfare. Instead they felt it meant support for people in real need and support for those who are helping them. In other words, it spoke of decency and not socialism. This has helped me point out to my colleagues that when we spent so much effort publically disavowing the term it left us appearing as uncaring or even crass.

Misunderstanding poverty

The result of all of this is that we have ceded this area to the left who have for too long set the terms of the debate and correspondingly willed the means. The consequences in my country are all too obvious. Thirteen years of Labour rule demonstrated how the left's approach is grounded in a very narrow understanding of what poverty is, and how it can be solved. Policy-makers became fixated with levels of income, rather than asking why people were living in poverty.

A poverty line became the benchmark by which all policy had to be measured. Yet in reality this line told us nothing about the root causes of problems. According to this approach, poverty was simply about a lack of money – and so the solution they pursued became income transfers through benefit payment increases, tax credits and a growing welfare system.

Worse still this fuelled a short-term political approach to government, for by measuring poverty in such an arbitrary way, politicians could tweak welfare payments to increase income for narrow groups and apparently 'lift' some people out of poverty. Superficial headline victories were hailed with a wave of a pen or a catchy ministerial initiative. But a few extra pounds in the pocket didn't actually change people's lives or give them opportunity.

Does anyone honestly believe that increasing a family's welfare payments slightly will mean their children are more likely to form stable and healthy relationships, achieve at school or find a job as an adult? Imagine, for a moment, an alcoholic mother living with two young daughters. Would those children's lives change by giving their mother more money? You'll change nothing for those children unless you also transform their mother's life.

The inadequacy of the previous UK government's approach was borne out by statistics. More than £150 billion has been spent on a system of targeted tax credits since 2003, in many cases with the aim of pushing families with children just above the poverty line. But progress was weak at best and by the time Labour left office, income inequality had reached record levels. And perhaps worse, the poorest groups in society went backwards.

So we should be clear: Income matters, but the root causes of poverty and the *source* of income matter more.

Five pathways to poverty

Dealing with the root causes of poverty rather than its symptoms was the reason I established the Centre for Social Justice, an independent think-tank. From the outset I spent a great deal of time in the UK's most disadvantaged neighbourhoods asking questions and seeking to understand what life was like in those seemingly forgotten places.

In the unseen chaos of dysfunctional homes and schools, I met a section of British society that had been completely left behind. I saw the poor healthcare, the discarded needles in vandalised playgrounds, the boarded windows and broken streetlights. Crime terrified families, but it also sucked in too many people who lived on these estates. Almost everything these people knew and experienced suggested government and society had given up on them.

Yet in the heart of many of these communities were voluntary community groups led by inspiring people – they held the secret of what leads people into poverty. It was that knowledge that shaped our definition of the five pathways to poverty:

Family breakdown.

Educational failure.

Severe personal debt.

Drug and alcohol addiction.

Welfare dependency – often characterised by intergenerational worklessness.

They are interconnected and move from generation to generation. A child who experiences family breakdown is more likely to fail at school. A child who fails at school is less likely to find employment and more likely to be dependent on benefits. A person on benefits, living on a very low income, is more likely to be in debt. And debt is one of the main causes of family breakdown.

The flicker of hope

Those who shaped the definition of the pathways to poverty were working in communities that the state simply failed to reach. They are ordinary people doing extraordinary things. Where the state had no answers, I think of courageous rehabilitation pioneers taking the most damaged heroin addicts into full recovery. I think of the unique residential charity fostering entire families and saving children from the black hole of Britain's care system and the youth workers offering violent gang members a way out.

These people and countless others like them are saving and transforming the lives of those cut adrift. By their success they prove, beyond any doubt at all, that beating poverty is about changing lives, not just giving people more money. By seizing their second chance, those they helped showed that most people will do the right thing if given an opportunity.

This gets to the heart of why Conservatives should embrace social justice. Instinctively, we understand that it is better to trust people because generally they do the right thing by themselves and their families. In this I believe society is governed by a dynamic of collective self-interest. As we grow, our horizons and values are shaped by education, relationships and community.

In this natural process as we develop from being single to being engaged in relationships, we move from self-interest to collective self-interest. Social policy has to grasp this to succeed, yet the potential of people to change their outcomes is something the left has often rejected. Too many such governments have sought to remove that freedom, seeing the poorest like children in need of direction, in so doing, extending their dependency on the state by degrees.

An un-ambitious left: the welfare legacy

My role in the UK's coalition government has brought me face-to-face with the legacy of static public policy. In May 2010, when I became Secretary of State for Work and Pensions, I inherited a broken welfare system. It was a system so dysfunctional and perverse that poverty had become the only possibility for many caught up in it. It was absurdly complex – more than 30 different types of benefit were governed by a maze of rules, regulations and disincentives. Officials and claimants were equally bemused by it.

For too many benefit claimants, choosing to take up work was seen as a poor choice. That is because someone moving into part-time work would find that they could end up losing even as much as 95 per cent of what they earned – due to high tax rates and punitive levels of benefit withdrawal. The result became an inflexible system which no longer encourages someone to seek work.

Today, the benefit system must recognise that the decision to take work, for the majority of people, is fundamentally a practical one. The effort you make in finding employment should be financially rewarding, yet the British welfare system assumes the poorest people would take work even when it clearly didn't pay. I suspect none of us would work for 90 per cent tax rates, especially if we could earn reasonable money for no effort at all, but that is what the system does in the UK.

This has resulted in intergenerational worklessness becoming a logical choice for too many in Britain. Despite record economic growth in the UK economy – 63 successive quarters of it – some 4.5 million people of working age were living on out of work benefits before the recent recession in the UK even started. Over one million have been on out of work benefits for more than 10 years and, most inexcusable of all, almost two million UK children live in households where no one works.

In parallel with the lack of financial incentive to take work, there was poorly targeted help for those who were expected to look for work. Welfare-to-work schemes were too often measured by process and outputs, such as the number of people entering and completing programmes, rather than outcomes, such as whether jobseekers were entering and staying in work. Support tended to be state-run, clunky and impersonal. All this meant we were failing those in the system, not to mention the taxpayers whose money was poured in to prop it up.

Reforming welfare and rebuilding society

I believe we have begun to steer a new course for welfare and social justice. We have launched the biggest system shake up since the Second World War. At the heart of this is the Universal Credit, a single integrated welfare payment which will replace a number of benefits and tax credits. Not only will this be simpler for claimants to navigate, it will be designed to make work pay at any number of hours.

Claimants will have a "disregard" – the amount of money they are allowed to earn before their benefits are withdrawn – and then a "taper rate" – which determines the rate at which the Universal

Credit is withdrawn as they increase their hours. This taper rate will be set at around 65 per cent for every claimant at every hour of work. No overlapping tapers, no cliff edges, just clear incentives to move into work.

We anticipate that the move to the Universal Credit could move almost one million people out of poverty. Critically, the gains from the change will overwhelmingly accrue to those in the bottom half of the income distribution.

Getting the incentives right is vital, but we also have to get people ready for work who have been out of work for some time. This isn't about skilling them up with some government inspired skills programme, but about building their confidence, helping them to present themselves and sell themselves. That's what our new Work Programme is doing.

In developing this Programme we have taken a great deal of interest in Australia's welfare to work schemes. I was especially keen to learn from your pioneering transition, launched by the Liberal government in 1998, from state-run employment services to voluntary and private sector provision, through the Jobs Network and now Job Services Australia.

As a country Britain has taken too long to understand the basic message that we shouldn't be so concerned with who delivers support or how they do it, but whether what they do actually *works*. We should be relentlessly focussed on outcomes, and that's what the Work Programme is about. We're contracting with the best in the public, private and voluntary sectors, paying them almost entirely for the results they achieve in getting people into work – and then keeping them there.

It's a single programme, but – as in Australia – we are using a system of differential pricing to make sure there is support for the hardest to help. If you help someone who has spent 10 years on sickness and disability benefits to find a job you'll get a much higher payment than if you help a typical jobseeker. Keep them in work for two years and you'll get the biggest payout. All of this is about changing lives and rewarding personal responsibility.

We are trying to build on what is best about the voluntary sector – those leaders I talked about earlier. A large proportion of the Prime and Sub-Prime Providers in the Work Programme are drawn from organisations from the voluntary sector. These are so often the organisations which have the knowledge, skills and experience to make a real difference to people's chances of finding work.

Underscoring all of this is a simple system of sanctions should someone refuse to cooperate. If they work with us we will help get the claimant into work but refuse and they will lose benefits. This is part of our contract with the taxpayer who is also part of this process, as it is taxpayers who pay for it.

Disability reforms

There is a third change we have to make if we are to enable all households to benefit from work. We have to reform our system of support for those groups that have been written off on inactive benefits for too long, particularly many disabled people. The demand for our main disability benefit has risen by 40 per cent for children. But we know that there are many disabled people who can work and want to do so, and it is completely unacceptable to leave them written off on benefits.

That's why we're moving to a model that is about asking what people can do, rather than focussing on what they can't, with regular objective assessments of everyone on incapacity benefits to assess changing conditions. Those who are ready and able to work will be moved onto Jobseeker's Allowance – our system of Unemployment Benefits. Those with a sickness or disability that affects their ability to work will be moved onto a more supportive benefit – the Employment and Support Allowance. Where their condition makes it difficult to even take steps towards work they will receive unconditional support at the highest rate.

We are taking a similar approach to Disability Living Allowance. Because it is available in and out of work this is not a question of work support. But it is about introducing a clearer and more regular assessment, one which looks more carefully at how a condition affects someone's life. We have to adopt a much more positive and proactive approach to disability, breaking a culture which sees people as fundamentally static.

Strengthening families

We are taking the same approach to lone parents, another group who have been unfairly written off. In the past little distinction was made between those whose caring responsibilities precluded them from doing any work at all, and those who were able to work within certain parameters. Prior to November 2008 lone parents could claim inactive benefits – known as Income Support – until their youngest child was 16. Now as a result of the changes we are making it will be reduced to five. Every household that can work should have work.

This is a welfare reform package which has its roots in conservatism. It is about trusting people and giving them a chance to build better futures.

All of this brings me to one of the most important issues facing society – that of the growing levels of family breakdown. Family breakdown in the UK is at historically high levels. For too long policy makers have ignored the effect of dysfunctional family formation on the character of communities and the future prospects of the children growing up in them. During my time at the Centre for Social Justice I determined that it was the role of government that we did what we could to change the scale of the levels of family breakdown that we now experience. What is vital is to ensure that government creates a level playing field for people as they form families.

One of the favoured attacks of the establishment left is that to do anything in this area is to unfairly favour married families. They are wrong. Yet what we have witnessed over the last decade or so is not neutrality in government policy towards family formations, particularly marriage, but what in effect amounts to an assault on the whole idea of marriage and long term commitment. While I accept that the state has no business lecturing people how to live their lives, it does though have a duty to at least be fair to those who choose to make sacrifices so that their children can be brought up in a stable and loving home.

I am someone who believes in following the evidence and the work of the CSJ shows what happens to children's outcomes when families break down. Armed with that evidence, we need to do much more to help people stabilise and form their relationships. It is clear that people respond to incentives and disincentives – and currently in the UK there is a damaging financial discouragement to couple formation, despite its stable outcomes for children. That's why I intend that our welfare reforms make an impact on the couple penalty where it matters most – amongst families on the lowest incomes.

Alongside that the Prime Minister has made it clear that we will, in this Parliament, recognise marriage in the tax system.

Conclusion

I don't come here to give advice or lecture you about strategy, nor do you need me to. But I do say the message on welfare reform should be more than just a story of cuts. As I have outlined, our life-changing message as Conservatives has never been more necessary.

Several years ago there was a deep need for change in Britain's Conservative Party. We had suffered major election defeats and had become out of touch. As leader I began a process of thinking anew about social reform and the need to reconnect with the aspirations of the British people – particularly those who had been let down by failed government. Through the work of the Centre for Social Justice, a tired debate about poverty and social justice has been radically reinvigorated. Instead of a stilted and often shallow debate about cuts versus spending, the real debate now centres on the question of how reform can achieve life transformation.

But isn't that what conservatives have always been about? Helping people to take control of their lives and strive to meet their aspirations is an optimistic message of a society where no one is discarded and no one is left behind. That is surely our true tradition.

The second John Howard Lecture was delivered in Sydney on 26 July 2011 entitled "Welfare Reform: investing in life change".

Acknowledgements

The Menzies Research Centre extends its thanks to contributors Henry Ergas, Kelly O'Dwyer, Rebecca Weisser and Alex Scaife.

Many thanks to Bill Leak for permission to reproduce his cartoon.

Our thanks to Mannkal Economic Education Foundation for its assistance in arranging Alex Scaife's internship at the Menzies Research Centre and Centre for Independent Studies in early 2015 that resulted in his contribution. Thanks to Greg Lindsay and the staff at the CIS for assistance in republishing Scaife's article.

The MRC is indebted to Anthony Cappello at Connor Court and editor Michael Gilchrist for their work in publishing the volume at short notice, and to the MRC Deputy Director Kay Gilchrist for her diligent logistical and production work.

Our thanks to Heather Henderson for permission to publish a page from her father Sir Robert Menzies' notebook and to the National Library of Australia for assistance in reproduction.

Nick Cater
Executive Director
Menzies Research Centre
June 2015